GUZOWSKI
522-76-4980

Conflict Analysis
Models and Resolutions

North-Holland Series in
SYSTEM SCIENCE AND ENGINEERING
Andrew P. Sage, *Editor*

1	**Wismer and Chattergy**	Introduction to Nonlinear Optimization: A Problem Solving Approach
2	**Sutherland**	Societal Systems: Methodology, Modeling, and Management
3	**Šiljak**	Large-Scale Dynamic Systems
4	**Porter et al.**	A Guidebook for Technology Assessment and Impact Analysis
5	**Boroush et al.**	Technology Assessment: Creative Futures
6	**Rouse**	Systems Engineering Models of Human–Machine Interaction
7	**Sengupta**	Decision Models in Stochastic Programming: Operational Methods of Decision Making Under Uncertainty
8	**Chankong and Haimes**	Multiobjective Decision Making: Theory and Methodology
9	**Jamshidi**	Large Scale Systems: Modeling and Control
10	**Sage**	Economic Systems Analysis
11	**Fraser and Hipel**	Conflict Analysis: Models and Resolutions